**business**buddies

# successful
## strategies for
# growth

For further success in all aspects of
business, be sure to read these other
businessbuddies books:

**business**buddies

# successful
## strategies for
# growth

Ken Lawson, M.A., Ed.M.

**BARRON'S**

First edition for the United States, its territories and dependencies, and Canada
published 2006 by Barron's Educational Series, Inc.

Conceived and created by
Axis Publishing Limited
8c Accommodation Road
London NW11 8ED
www.axispublishing.co.uk

Creative Director: Siân Keogh
Editorial Director: Anne Yelland
Design: Sean Keogh, Simon de Lotz
Managing Editor: Conor Kilgallon
Production: Jo Ryan, Cécile Lerbière

NOTE: The opinions and advice expressed in this book are intended as a guide only. The publisher
and author accept no responsibility for any loss sustained as a result of using this book.

*All inquiries should be addressed to:*
Barron's Educational Series, Inc.
250 Wireless Boulevard
Hauppauge, New York 11788
**www.barronseduc.com**

Library of Congress Control No: 2005936257

ISBN-13: 978-0-7641-3516-3
ISBN-10: 0-7641-3516-3

Printed and bound in China
9 8 7 6 5 4 3 2 1

# contents

# Introduction

You've worked hard to establish your business and run it successfully. You've put in long hours and many months, or years, of energy and effort to make it work. You've given the business your creativity, imagination, persistence, and courage to take it to the level of success you've attained. And now you're confronting two unavoidable questions: What's the next level of success, and how do I reach it?

*Successful Strategies for Growth* provides insight and ideas that will help you tackle those questions and wrestle them to the ground. What happens when business levels off, or hits a plateau and can go no further? Often, part of the dilemma many business owners face is that they remain too close to their own enterprise to clearly see what they are doing and evaluate their numerous options for growth. The ideas and guidelines in these pages will help you avoid that situation by showing you, in clear, easy-to-read language, the range of growth-oriented options and courses of action available to you.

You'll begin just as you did when you were putting together your initial business plan—by assessing your current performance. Take fresh stock of how your business is progressing. Review its track record over time. And look objectively at your propensity for managing risk.

Then, create and develop a vision for business growth. In these pages you'll find guidelines for assessing your growth options and their practicality. You'll evaluate the possibility of internal, "organic" growth and weigh it against the prospects of collaborative, external growth. And, you'll take a fresh, growth-oriented look at your customers, your competitors, your employees, and your "go-it-alone" option.

In Chapters 3 and 4, *Successful Strategies for Growth* details a broad range of specific options for business expansion and progression. Read about mergers and acquisitions and how to approach the decisions that relate to each. Find out about the many kinds of joint ventures and partnerships, from strategic alliances and partnerships to joint venture

# Introduction continued

companies. And learn about such options as licensing, franchising, supply partnerships, and how to ensure that your joint venture relationship is one that is a success from the start.

Lest you leap before you look, *Successful Strategies for Growth* provides helpful tips and advice on weighing the benefits and risks of collaboration. The deliberate, step-by-step organization of these ideas and insights will help you get out of your own thinking, to achieve the distance and objectivity you need in order to make a sound decision about growing your business.

Lastly, as you move closer to action, you'll find ideas and information on planning for growth. Learn why innovation is your strongest ally, and why customer feedback is invaluable. Understand how knowledge—of your employees, your product, and your customers— defines your business success. Find out about outsourcing, training, choosing your management team, and other options for your new, expanded business.

Growth and expansion are issues that confront all successful businesses at one time or another. And while they can seem like daunting, intimidating goals, they are first and foremost indicators of success. *Sucessful Strategies for Growth* offers ideas and guidelines for you to aim at a new, even higher level of business success.

Ken Lawson, M.A., Ed.M.

Career management counselor and author

Instructor, School of Continuing and Professional Studies

New York University

# 1

assessing current performance

# How is your business progressing?

You are sure that your business is progressing satisfactorily. Your cash flow forecasts are in line with your accounts, and the profit and loss account is looking very healthy with a good return on the investments made. Your ratios all have the right look about them.

## ARE YOU REALLY DOING WELL?

**1** How do you compare with similar businesses of the same size?

**2** Are you satisfying your customers' needs, or are they sometimes being let down by your delivery dates or by the inability of some of your own suppliers to meet your requirements?

**3** How many times have you not been able to accept an order from a customer because you could not meet the required delivery time or because the items they wanted were not standard to your product range?

**4** Now is the time to really assess your current performance and to assess whether you can match or outpace your nearest competitors, and how.

# Benchmarking

Benchmarking is a way of comparing key elements of your business either against a known standard or by comparison with another company of a similar size and performance.

**1** It compares costs and productivity and looks at customer service and, very importantly, your levels of staff retention and turnover.

**2** It enables you to form an overview of your company's strengths and weaknesses, its opportunities, and those things that threaten it.

**3** It shows what changes you could initiate to make your business more successful.

When you make comparisons with other businesses, your own business will be rendered more sharply in focus. In addition, by gaining a better understanding of the issues facing the business, you will be better placed to develop plans for the future.

You will need to choose your comparator carefully since setting your targets too high or too low will give a false picture of your own capabilities, with the result that you might overstretch or underachieve, both of which are undesirable.

# Benchmarking continued

Some of the main headings for benchmarking are:

**1** Costs: production costs, overheads, and marketing.

**2** Sales and turnover: By comparison with a business of a similar size, are your sales figures higher or lower?

**3** Pricing: How competitive are your prices?

**4** Staff retention: Do you have a high turnover of staff? What are their exit comments?

**5** Products: How do you rate on quality and general appearance?

6    Customer base: Are you reliant on just a few customers?

7    Key performance indicators

Benchmarking should be considered an on-going exercise and not just an appraisal that will happen only once. That way, the health of your business is always being monitored and any remedial action can be taken before things become acute.

**assessing current performance**

# What should you benchmark?

There are two major ways to benchmark, internal and competitive. In the former, you measure activities within your own business to find the most productive areas and which products are most cost-effective. In the latter, you try to compare with a known competitor in terms of price, market share, and quality. While benchmarking can help you to assess every part of your business, concentrate on those areas that will bring the most benefit.

**1** Are there any areas that are not achieving their full potential?

**2** Could sales improve?

**3** Are you carrying too much stock of unsold items?

**4** Is there too much wastage in the production cycle?

These are all "hard facts" of your business performance. But how about the "soft facts"?

**START WITH STAFF RELATIONS.**

**1** Can your staff identify training that would help them to be more efficient?

**2** Can they suggest any ways to improve performance?

**3** Do they feel part of the business?

And do not forget to check that suppliers are satisfied with their relationship with the company.

# What should you benchmark? continued

Benchmarking within your own company is a fairly straightforward process and involves receiving reports from various departments. Trying to benchmark with competitors can be more difficult as companies are not usually willing to divulge sensitive or confidential information to their competitors.

Make use of surveys carried out by trade organizations and some government departments. The statistics are regularly published in trade journals and on government, industry, and news websites.

There are external organizations that will discuss your requirements with you and then draw up a program for obtaining the information against agreed targets. Information on companies offering this service can also be obtained from the Internet.

No matter how thorough your benchmarking process might be, it will be futile if you are not committed to act upon its findings. The process might highlight one or two areas of your business that are in need of attention and improvement, and this must be implemented in order to be effective in the long term.

**1** Always remember that the objectives of companies differ.

**2** You may be targeting your sales to a "niche market," whereas a competitor may have a much wider spread.

**3** You may concentrate on one part of the country, whereas a competitor may cover a much larger territory. These factors can skew the findings.

This should not be a one-time-only activity but should be ongoing.

# Reviewing your performance

External realities and internal performance

It is unusual for any business to stand still. Once established, there are often various reasons why the business should grow. Customer satisfaction, investment in research and development, more efficient use of resources, all of these need to be assessed. So now is the time to review your position against the business plan.

**1** What is your position in the market and are you competing in the right markets?

**2** Are you using your resources to their maximum advantage and what other resources do you need to continue to expand?

**3** Although it might seem a strange question, ask yourself "what do I actually do"?

**4** What is my core business?

**5** What is it about my product or service that makes it different from similar products and services in the marketplace?

**6** Could it be improved? If so, how?

**7** Is there anything of a similar nature that I could provide and market?

The answers to these questions can be quite enlightening and can provide you with a signpost for future growth. There is no point in trying to grow your business if the market is unable to absorb the increase in output of a particular product or service.

# Reviewing your performance continued

It is not only an external review that you need to undertake but also a critical assessment of your internal procedures.

**1** Are your quality control systems effective?

**2** Are your direct costs under control?

**3** Have your overheads risen recently, and if they have, for what reason?

**4** Would new production methods or new materials reduce manufacturing costs and improve the product?

**5** Would more up-to-date methods improve your service?

Once you have completed this assessment of your business you will have a good idea if you are still going in the right direction and working efficiently.

This in itself might lead to an increase in the size and output of the business without the need to consider some of the available strategies for growth.

**assessing current performance**

# SWOT analysis

One useful analytical tool to aid the business review is the SWOT analysis. SWOT stands for Strengths, Weaknesses, Opportunities, and Threats. It requires an honest and critical review of the business under these four headings listed above. It takes the form of a grid pattern.

| POSITIVE | NEGATIVE |
| --- | --- |
| STRENGTHS<br>OPPORTUNITIES | WEAKNESSES<br>THREATS |

Strengths and weaknesses are usually internal functions of the business, whereas opportunities and threats are external factors. Once identified you can work to capitalize on the strengths of your business and seek to minimize the effects of the weaknesses. It is possible for opportunities and threats to be counter-productive. For example, an opportunity that you identify could, if capitalized on by a competitor, become a threat. Of course, the reverse also applies.

Another useful tool is the PESTEL analysis. This looks at the external influences of Politics, Economics, Society, Technology, Environment, and Law upon your company, product, or service. These influences can have a major effect upon the way the market perceives and receives your output.

assessing current performance

# PESTEL analysis

Looking at each of the headings will help you to understand the relevance of each to your business.

## 1 POLITICAL

- Governments always seek to try to improve the general economic situation during their term of office to fund the legislation proposed in their election manifesto.

- This may have an effect upon the business opportunities that have been planned.

- Governments may make trade agreements with other countries, which your company must honor.

- This may change if a successive government decides to enter into a different agreement with their trading partners.

- Other countries' political decisions are also likely to have an effect upon growth strategy if overseas markets are being considered.

## 2 ECONOMIC

■ Export markets can be at the mercy of world economic trends.

■ Changes in bank rates and currency exchange rates could make your product too expensive in certain countries, and this will have a major effect upon sales forecasts.

■ Imports of raw material from abroad can also vary in price and can cause production costs to rise.

■ Competitors may not be affected in the same way if they source from other areas.

# PESTEL analysis continued

**3** SOCIAL

- This heading can cover many things that will have an effect on your chosen strategies.

- Fashions change, and the customers will want to move with trends and styles so that the products that have always been "best-sellers" could fall out of favor.

- The way in which people live and spend their free and working time can also impact upon choice.

- Demographics will influence projections for growth in certain areas, not only at home but also worldwide.

- Improved life expectancy may have an impact on your market share.

- Increased spending power also needs to be taken into consideration.

**4** TECHNOLOGICAL

■ Advances in technology in many businesses need to be forecast if products or services are to be competitive.

■ Look at the advances in IT products over the last three or four years to see how manufacturers in this field have had to remain abreast of the latest developments.

■ Many companies did not keep pace, and once-famous names are now out of business.

**5** ENVIRONMENTAL

- The conservation of the environment is now high on the list of requirements of the majority of the nations on this planet.

- Emissions of harmful waste products have to be carefully controlled, and regulations covering new buildings are introduced to implement this.

- Expansion of existing facilities will need to conform with these rules and should be considered in growth planning. The use of certain materials in manufacture and some fossil fuels will also have an impact upon future plans.

**6** LEGAL

■ As more emerging countries are developing their manufacturing industries and thereby developing new and improved products, there is an increase in patent protection in these countries.

■ We now have to be more aware of the infringement possibilities that arise.

■ Conversely, we must ensure that any patents we own are up to date and infringements are monitored for our protection.

■ Worldwide protection from a single source is still some way in the future.

■ Trading groups and economic communities impose legal restrictions on various forms of trading, and these have to be monitored to ensure compliance with regulations.

Whenever you are planning growth, it is advisable to look at these six headings to see if there have been changes since the last analysis.

# Five forces analysis

A third analytical tool is Michael Porter's Five Forces Analysis. This helps the marketer to contrast the competitive environment. It looks at the five key areas that will affect success in entering a market. These are;

**1** THE THREAT OF ENTRY
- The existence of any barriers to entry
- Economies of scale
- Brand equity
- Switching costs
- Expected retaliation
- Cost advantages

**2** THE POWER OF BUYERS
- Buyer volume
- Bargaining leverage
- Availability of existing substitute products
- Buyer price sensitivity
- Price of total purchase

**3** THE POWER OF SUPPLIERS
- Cost differences
- Substitute inputs
- Supplier-to-company ratio
- Supplier costs relative to selling price
- Volume levels

**4** THE THREAT OF SUBSTITUTES
- Perceived level of product differentiation
- Price of substitutes

**5** COMPETITIVE RIVALRY
- Threat of new entrants
- Power of buyers
- Power of suppliers
- Threat of substitute products
- Industry overcapacity
- Brand loyalty

# Key questions

You should be constantly asking, "Where is our business?" and the following key questions will provide the answers.

**1** Is our business plan up-to-date? We should constantly review the plan against our progress and achievements to ensure we are on course.

**2** Are all of our procedures efficient? Could any of the processes that we use be operated in a more efficient manner? Are costs escalating or failing to meet our quality standards? Are they still providing customer satisfaction?

**3** Can we identify areas for improvement? The answers to the previous question will show where these areas could be.

4    Is our SWOT analysis still valid? Have our strengths and weaknesses changed, are the threats still there, and are we meeting the opportunities we identified? New entries could appear in each of the headings, and this should change the way in which we run the business.

5    Are we still on line for growth strategy? Has anything happened, either internally or externally that will alter our strategic planning? If it has, what steps can we take to bring us back to plan?

**KEY QUESTIONS**

**assessing current performance**

# Managing risk

Every business faces risks every day. The definition of a business risk is "the probability of an event and its consequences." Managing risk is identifying what could go wrong, deciding on those that are important, and finding strategies to be able to deal with them. An effective risk management policy is a powerful antidote to business failure.

**THE RISK MANAGEMENT PROCESS INVOLVES:**

**1** Identifying risk

**2** Assessing probability

**3** Establishing systems to deal with the consequences

**4** Monitoring

The risk management process will allow you to anticipate what may go wrong and to take preventative action. In addition, it affords these benefits:

1 It will help in the allocation of financial resources.

2 It will highlight any problem areas that might be looming in the various processes of both production and distribution.

3 It is essential to have a risk management procedure in place if you are planning to expand the business in either new products or new markets.

# Managing risk continued

The main areas of risk are concerned with Finance, Operations, and Strategy. You will already have established financial systems to record and manage the day-to-day cashflows but there are occurrences that are unexpected and which can have a dramatic effect on your ability to function.

1   What would be the effect if a major customer ran into financial difficulty and could not pay, or worse, ceased trading completely?

2   What would happen if a breakdown in one of your processes meant that production, and therefore sales, was delayed for a period of time?

3   If your business is dependent on outside finance, such as loans or mortgages, what would be the effect of an increase in interest rates?

4   If you are exporting to a customer who will pay in a currency other than your own, what will be the effect of a change in the exchange rate?

THE WAY IN WHICH YOUR BUSINESS OPERATES NEEDS TO BE EXAMINED.

**1** How long is the supply chain and have you got an alternative source?

**2** How heavily do you depend on IT and is there a backup system in case of a fault?

**3** Are there any health and safety regulations that could be altered and would mean major changes?

If any of these are identified, then the risks should be prioritized and provision made for such an event.

# Managing risk continued

It is obvious that the most important risks are those that should be given the highest priority, but how can you evaluate the risk?

**1** Consider both the probability that something will happen and its consequences.

**2** Make a list of all the risks that you have identified, and rank both the consequence and the probability: high, medium, or low.

**3** Any risk with a high/high rating needs urgent attention, while low/low should not be a priority item.

**4** If you prioritize risks in this way, you can direct both time and money toward the most important.

THERE ARE FOUR WAYS OF MANAGING EACH RISK:

**1** Accept it because the cost of eliminating it is too high.

**2** Transfer it by means of a form of insurance.

**3** Reduce it by taking some action that will minimize its chance of occurring.

**4** Eliminate it by changing the process completely.

Again it must be stressed that risk management is not a one-time-only exercise. It is a continuous management policy.

# Managing risk checklist

**1** Identify where the risk might occur. ☐

**2** Assess what the risk could be. ☐

**3** Assess the probability of a risk occurring. ☐

**4** Establish a system for dealing with the risk. ☐

**5** Monitor the risk. ☐

**6** Establish whether the risk has been eliminated or reduced. ☐

**7** Establish if the risk has moved to a different area. ☐

**CHECKLIST**

2

a vision for growth

# Assess your options for growth

Now that you have completed a full assessment of your business in its current state and you feel confident that you have all departments and areas working efficiently and under control, it is time to look to the future.

**1** What is your vision for the future?

**2** Does your business plan offer a realistic guide as to your future direction?

**3** Do you just want to consolidate your current position or do you want to find ways to make the business grow?

Starting a business can involve lots of hard work, courageous decisions, and not a few risks, and it may seem a good idea to just sit back, relax, and enjoy the benefits of all your efforts.

**1** Can you afford to do nothing?

**2**   While you do nothing, your competitors will be growing and taking your market share—this will seriously damage your business's future.

**3**   To ensure that your business remains a success, it is time to identify your options for growth.

Growth options can be divided into two categories, internal and external.

**1**   Internal growth or growth that can be achieved within your own business will involve increasing market share or diversification.

**2**   External growth will involve joining forces with another business, either by merging with or acquiring another company or by forming a partnership or joint venture with another business.

External growth strategies will be considered in Chapters 3 and 4.

**a vision for growth**

# Business strategy

Business strategy was defined by Newburry, Zeira, and Yeheskel as: "...the determination of the basic long-term goals and objectives of an enterprise, and the adoption of courses of action and the allocation of resources necessary for carrying out these goals." The necessity of thoroughly evaluating a business to get a clear picture of its strengths, weaknesses, opportunities, and threats was discussed in Chapter 1. This will provide important insights into the type of growth strategy that best suits the business for the immediate and long-term future.

## INTERNAL GROWTH

**1** Are there ways in which you can improve the efficiency of the business?

**2** The use of a system of statistical process control will show if your processes are working correctly.

**3**   Could the quality of the product or service be improved?

**4**   Adopting a system of Total Quality Management (TQM) may effect a change to your end product.

**5**   Are costs as competitive as they can be?

**6**   If these checks are carried out successfully, then it is reasonable to expect that the business will grow by organic growth. This will make the business more competitive.

The first thing to establish is whether you can increase your share of the market. To do this you would have to take customers from your competitors or attract new customers. You have to understand your customer base and that of your competitors.

## CUSTOMERS

**1** Who are your existing customers?

**2** Are there any that you have not yet targeted?

**3** Are there any that no longer do business with you? Why?

**4** Do any of them buy from your competitors? Why?

**5** Do they have instant, alternative choices?

COMPETITORS

**1** What are their strengths? Can you match them?

**2** Have you lost customers to them?

**3** What do they do better than you do?

# Business strategy continued

OURSELVES

**1** What is our sustainable competitive advantage?

**2** What do we do that is better than our competitors?

**3** What is our unique selling point?

**4** How will growth affect our pricing, marketing, and service levels?

Before increasing output by increasing the capacity of your processes, you need to ensure that there will be a market for your proposed additional products. Many companies have increased output in the anticipation that the market will follow, only to find that there is a downturn or that a competitor has already improved performance.

**a vision for growth**

# Diversification

Many small businesses can grow by diversifying into other related products or services. For example, an office stationery supplier might decide to add a range of computer consumables to its portfolio. This could result in existing customers now buying these items as well.

Diversification can occur in different forms, such as:

**1** Selling similar or related new products to existing customers.

**2** Selling existing products into new markets, even overseas.

**3** Selling new products to new markets.

Before deciding on diversification, take the following actions:

**1** Thoroughly research both markets and customers for the new product or service.

**2** Decide on a clear development strategy.

**3** Do a trial run with a limited output of prototypes to test the market before committing to the new product or service.

**4** Ensure that the internal departments and outside suppliers can maintain a steady throughput to provide continuity.

It would be damaging if the customer orders are plentiful but the supply of the product or service is intermittent.
In the early stages, diversification will rate highly in your risk assessment program, and in order to mitigate some of the risk, it is advisable to try to secure customer orders or commitments in advance of stepping up production.

# The "go-it-alone" option

One option for growth that falls between internal and external growth is the go-it-alone option.

**1** The major benefit of this option is that the business retains full control with all profits (or losses) retained in-house, as are all designs, manufacturing, and marketing knowledge.

**2** It presupposes the business is in good financial and operational "health" and that it can supply all of the necessary resources to launch and supply into the market.

**3** Although the title of the option suggests that all the work is carried out in-house, this will depend on the manufacturing strategy that is operating within the company.

**4** Even though most businesses would like to keep control of all the processes involved in manufacturing their products or the services they offer, economics and common sense decree that some processes are best performed by outside contractors. This is referred to as a "make or buy policy" and will determine where work is performed.

**5** The work of the contractors is controlled to advantage through agreements and contracts.

# The practicalities of growth

There are many resources that need to be considered when deciding to grow the business. Among these are:

## FINANCE
It is unlikely that the business will have generated large reserves of cash that will enable expansion to be paid for from internal sources.

- It will take time for the proposed growth to generate sufficient income to pay for the increased facilities.

- It is necessary to consider where the investment needed to grow is to be obtained, how much is needed, and when it will be needed.

- Prepare a detailed cash flow plan to show when the financial input is needed. When the investment has to be repaid, the forecast will show how soon this can be done.

## STAFF

Do you have sufficient staff to undertake the extra work, or will you need to employ more people?

- What skill levels are required and can they be found from within the current team?

- Will it be difficult to find such people?

- Will you need to set up training programs for current or new employees?

## PREMISES

Do you have sufficient room for the new production facilities and increased stock levels of both materials and finished parts?

- Will there be room for the additional staff that could be required?

- Will you still meet the relevant health and safety regulations?

## MARKETING

Can your current marketing arrangements cope with increased sales and the new product or service?

# The practicalities of growth continued

We have posed some questions regarding the availability of finance, staff, and premises. It is now necessary to look at sources of supply.

## FINANCE

■ Sources of finance will depend largely on the nature of the business.

■ If it is a limited liability company with shareholders, there could be the possibility of increasing the authorized capital and selling more shares to existing or new investors.

■ The ability to do this will depend upon the overall financial viability of the company.

■ If the capital is entirely your own or shared among family members, then asking all of the current investors to increase their holding might be a way forward.

■ Banks and investment companies might be prepared to advance loans on a "nonsecured" basis, but again this will depend upon the financial health of the business and the general economic climate.

■ There are people called "business angels" who look for well-managed companies, with a growth potential, in which to invest private capital, usually in return for a stake in the company.

In all of the above cases, it will be necessary to talk to your accountant before deciding on a course of action.

# The practicalities of growth continued

STAFF

■ If at all possible, promoting staff from within the company to meet the needs of an expanded business is recommended.

■ They are aware of company policies and procedures and will be known to you.

■ They may need to be trained for their new role and that can be done in-house, if necessary, by external training organizations or at seminars run by these companies.

■ It will be necessary to see that the salaries paid to these newly trained staff are commensurate with those in other companies; otherwise, the investment in staff training and development is likely to be lost to competitors.

■ If promoting from within is not possible, then recruitment must be considered. Dependent upon the seniority of the post is the type of recruitment.

■ For lower level positions, newspaper advertising is usually sufficient. For more senior positions, specialist recruitment bureaus or even "head-hunters" should be employed.

■ In any case, think carefully about the position(s) to be filled and plan ahead.

## PREMISES

- Part of your business plan should be the consideration of premises that are suitable for expansion.

- What space do you have at your current location for growth?

- Could a redesign of present facilities provide space?

- If it is necessary to find new premises, can you move all the operation to a new site, or will you maintain the current site?

- The question of logistics then has to be considered.

- In the current climate, IT and administrative affairs can be handled at different locations, but manufacturing processes often suffer if they are located at different sites.

# 3

mergers and acquisitions

# External forms of growth

Chapter 2 explored the way that a business can grow by paying attention to the internal affairs of the company, and how diversification can lead into new products and new markets. Chapter 2 also considered the possibility of a go-it-alone option, and this will be referred to again, but this chapter will concentrate on the various external forms of growth.

Could your business benefit from an acquisition or a merger? Again, you need to take a good look at the business to understand just where it is at the present time. What are the strengths that you can build on? What do you have that would make your company attractive to other companies? Are there areas of weakness in the business? Could these be strengthened by acquiring another company or merging your business with another?

**SOME OF THE QUESTIONS TO ASK ARE:**

**1** Should we obtain more quality staff with different skills?

**2** What do we know about our sector of the industry or service? Could we improve our business intelligence to our advantage?

**3** Is our business underperforming and, if so, in which area(s)?

**4** Can we access funds for further development without endangering the normal business cash flow?

**5** Could we access a wider customer base and increase our market share without outside help? How much would it cost in extra resources?

**6** Could we diversify into other products or service areas? What would be the long-term effects?

**7** Can we reduce our cost and overhead structure without damaging our product, service, or customer base? Would there be an adverse effect on performance and quality?

**8** What would be the effect if we could reduce the competition?

**9** Would "organic growth" take too long?

**mergers and acquisitions**

# Factors to consider

The answers to the questions posed on pp. 68–69 will be a good guide to future planning of the business. But a lot depends on how the management team sees the future of the company.

So what would be the reasons for considering growth either through a merger or by an acquisition?

**1** Bigger is better? Although the idea of becoming a major company may have its attractions, it is not always the best option. Sometimes being the only supplier in a niche market may offer opportunities that will create a business that will satisfy not only the market but also the aspirations of the owners.

**2** Image enhancement? It is certainly true that a well-known company that is a household name will attract a large customer base. It could also attract predators who might strip both assets and name, and the image will be lost forever.

**3** Market expansion? A good survey to see how much the market can and will absorb is a prerequisite to this form of growth, but a great deal depends on the type of product or service that you are supplying.

**4** Product range expansion? Merging with or acquiring another company whose products complement your own is a good way to increase market share without the expense of developing new products, introducing new production facilities, and expanding your own marketing department. It should also expand the customer base of both individual businesses.

**5** Diversification? Similar to product range expansion, should you wish to change the direction of the company, then this form of growth will provide a ready-made means of market entry without the worry and problems of setting up new facilities and establishing new markets.

The first two forms of external growth to be considered are mergers and acquisitions. They work in different ways, so will be considered separately.

# What is a merger?

The dictionary definition of a merger in the business or commercial context is "the combination of two or more companies, either by the creation of a new organization or by absorption by one of the others." The underlying logic of mergers is that the resulting enterprise will be stronger than the combined resources of the individual companies. This is described as synergy, and it offers more business possibilities. It also has the advantage that there will be less competition as a result of the merger, although this depends on the guidelines of a monopoly commission.

## WHAT ARE THE MAJOR ATTRIBUTES OF A TRUE MERGER?

**1**

**TEAMWORK**
The whole idea of a merger is to absorb both companies into an integrated whole so that each party contributes its own strengths to the overall project. The merging businesses will have recognized the assets each has to contribute and will work together to meld, as seamlessly as possible, into a more forceful whole unit. There should be no opposing views on the conduct of the new business. The future plans and strategies should have been established, and both parties should be able to direct their efforts into ensuring that these are performed efficiently and profitably.

## 2  SHARING

For the merger to be fully effective there should be no "them and us" attitude, and both workforces should integrate their skills and abilities for the benefit of the enlarged organization. Technology and processes should be shared so that full advantage may be made of the strengths that each of the parties brings to the merger.

# What is a merger? continued

## 3 NONDOMINATION

Regardless of the relative size of each of the companies, one company should not dominate the other. This could be most difficult to achieve especially where one company thinks that it has made the major input into the merger, either in resources or technical know-how. This is something that has to be established at the early stages of talks and possibly compensated for in some manner. Such a problem could arise if one of the partner companies already has a very high profile in the market.

## 4  MUTUAL BENEFIT

All parties to the merger must sink their personal ambitions for their own company into working for the mutual benefit of the new organization and use all of its assets to maximum effect. It is sometimes hard to realize that where there has been an unequal input of resources of various kinds, for example, finance, workforce, or customer base, there should not be disparity in the amount of return on these assets. All parties must work equally hard to ensure the success of the new business for it is from this success that the merger will grow and produce the desired results.

THE FINANCIAL STRUCTURE FOR A MERGER IS:

Company "A" shares ⟹

Company "B" shares ⟹

Company "C" shares

# Is the time right for a merger?

Ascertaining whether the time is right for a merger depends on the state of your business relative to the market and to the competition.

**1** Have you prepared a SWOT analysis of your organization to find your "business health"? ☐

**2** Will your strengths and opportunities combine to provide a springboard for expansion? ☐

**3** Do your weaknesses and threats demonstrate that you are vulnerable? ☐

**4** Does good market intelligence give you an idea of the state of your major competitor(s) in similar areas? ☐

**5** Have you looked at company reports or obtained credit rating/business references of your competitors?

**6** Can you find complementary matches in a likely company to see if a merger will be beneficial to both parties?

**7** Will both partners succeed to provide the synergy needed for a successful merger?

**8** Have you considered the state of the market; will a larger company increase its sales potential to a point greater than the sum of the individual parts?

CHECKLIST

# What is an acquisition?

Meaning "to gain possession of," the acquisition of all or parts of another business is an alternative method to develop or expand your own business.

**1** An acquisition is the most apposite option where you need specialist skills and knowledge or facilities for your own future development.

**2** This is a way of filling "holes" in a company's current or future strategy; it can be very successful as long as there is a good understanding of what the knowledge gaps are and how they can be filled effectively.

**3** As is the case with mergers, the questions posed on pp. 68–71 should be asked and answered, and the correct business fit must be achieved.

Most acquisitions involve businesses of unequal size with, usually, the larger or more powerful company purchasing or acquiring the smaller. In recent times, this has not always been the case, and examples can be found of relatively small companies buying out much larger ones, either to obtain resources or to gain additional assets to supplement those currently owned.

Such deals are usually financed quite heavily with loans and other deals and are often followed by a very vigorous pruning of parts of the acquisition to repay the financing involved. This is known as asset stripping and is rarely intended to achieve growth of an established business, but rather functions as a financial dealing that will generate cash for further enlargement.

# Hostile takeovers

Many acquisitions are known as "hostile takeovers" where the management of the company being purchased actively resists the unwanted overtures of the predator company.

**1** This often leads to serious management difficulties and enormous planned and unplanned costs.

**2** It can take several years (if at all) to see the benefits of such hostility and the planned and hoped for advantages of such growth to materialize.

**3** The costs involved with such an acquisition are usually extremely high, as there is little cooperation in trying to implement the necessary changes to both organizations.

When talking about mergers, such phrases as: "teamwork," "sharing," and "mutual benefit" are appropriate; some of the expressions used when considering hostile takeovers might be:

**1** "We have bought you."

**2** "Do as you are told."

**3** "Our way is best."

# Hostile takeovers continued

The phrases on p. 81 are obviously not the key words to a growth strategy that is going to benefit both the acquirer and the acquired, but a well-planned and targeted acquisition can enhance both companies' positions in the market. One of the keys to success is not to keep the newly purchased company at "arm's length" but to actively create value from the new relationship. A report by the University of Warwick Business School in the UK concluded that "76 percent of acquisitions involved little if any resource transfer, while 49 percent were simply left to stand-alone after the acquisition." These actions, or inactions, are a waste of money and time. The underlying idea of growth through acquisition is to utilize the resources you targeted at the investigation stage as quickly as possible to enable your own business to grow and flourish.

Before any acquisition (or merger), it is essential to establish that what you think you are acquiring is real and worthwhile and to use a process such as due diligence. This includes complete studies of the business you seek to acquire, which should be carried out by specialist, uninvolved, third parties, who look at every part of the business and report on its viability to meet the requirements you have set before you take irrevocable action.

In 1987, the British company Ferranti, a leading specialist in electric and electronic products, bought US group International Signal and Control (ISC) at a cost of $700 million.

ISC was claimed to be a very successful defense company that turned out to be nearly worthless. In consequence, Ferranti was financially crippled. This is a classic example of due diligence not being paid.

# Making the decision to acquire

**1** It is necessary, as a prerequisite to making an acquisition, to have established the strengths and weaknesses of your current business. Only then can you start to look for a business that will best complement your current position and help to grow your business.

**2** Will the proposed business meet your expectations?

**3** What type of business is it? Is it a private limited company, a public limited company, or a partnership?

**4** What is the location of the business? Does this cause any problems with logistics? Are there any local restrictions that might come into play should you need to transfer parts of the businesses between sites?

**5** Are there any well-established competitors that might affect your marketing?

**6** If the current owner(s) of the business seem very willing to sell, are there any "hidden reasons" for such willingness?

Remember the due diligence procedure mentioned earlier. Arriving at incisive answers to these questions represents the exemplary use of due diligence.

# Valuing the acquisition

There are several valuation methods that can be used, and it is always best to seek professional expert advice before making the final decision. To obtain an overview of how healthy the business might be, you should consider the following factors:

**1** The history of the business. How and when did it start? Has it always been in its current location?

**2** The current performance. What are its sales, turnover, and profit levels? Is there a rising or falling trend?

**3** The financial situation. Look at the cash flow, debtors and creditors, stock levels, assets, and liabilities.

**4** What is the condition of the premises? Are they freehold or leasehold? How long is the lease?

**5** Intangible assets. These are always difficult to measure, but they do provide an insight into the way that the company has been run. What is the company's reputation with its customers and suppliers? Has it changed recently? (This has to be established by talking to both.) Does the company own any patents or other intellectual property? Do they manufacture anything under license from another company? Can the license be transferred, if required?

**6** Employees. Remember that there may be state laws and union agreements regarding the transfer of undertakings and the treatment of existing employees.

**7** Once you have considered all of these factors, you can then decide how much you think the business is worth and how much you are prepared to offer, if you decide to proceed.

# Valuing the acquisition continued

THE FINANCIAL STRUCTURE OF AN ACQUISITION IS:

Company "C" shares

Company "A" shares

Larger company "A" shares

## WHAT CAN GO WRONG?

In 1999, the management group KPMG studied 700 mergers and acquisitions. Their conclusions found that:

■ 53 percent reduced the value of the companies.

■ 17 percent produced no added value.

■ Most "mergers" were acquisitions in disguise.

In 2003, a report issued by another group, Towers Perrin, indicated that there was a considerable increase in merger and acquisition activity, but surveys of companies concerned "still admit to a high failure rate."

■ 57 percent of "doomed deals" were caused by incompatible cultures in the companies involved.

■ In 42 percent of cases, a clash of management styles or egos was responsible for the failure.

# What can go wrong?

The extent and the quality of the planning and research done before a merger or acquisition deal is done will largely determine the outcome. There are occasions when situations will arise that are outside your control. It is worthwhile to consider the following situations and to prepare for them.

**THE DEAL COULD FAIL OR PROVE TO BE VERY EXPENSIVE IF:**

**1** Agreement cannot be reached on who should run the business in the case of a merger or, in the case of an acquisition, how long the previous management team will continue to remain involved. (It is usual to have some members of the team at the helm during the transition stage but judgment is required when this will cease.)

**2** Word gets out in the press that you are interested in merging or acquiring a particular business and a "bidding war" breaks out in which other determined parties are interested in buying into the business.

**3** Your own business performance suffers because you have to spend too long on the deal and the transition stages.

**4** Key people in either organization leave because of uncertainty.

**5** The expected savings in costs do not materialize.

# Successful mergers and acquisitions

**1** Do a company "health check." Examine every possible facet of the business.

**2** Discover if there any areas for improvement and prune out any waste.

**3** Complete an up-to-date SWOT analysis.

**4** Ensure that your strengths and opportunities support an external growth strategy.

**5** Weigh up the likely contenders for a merger/acquisition.

**6** Decide which strategy will be best for the company, bearing in mind that an acquisition can be a costly and sometimes bitter affair.

**7** Try to prevent plans for either form of growth being made public too soon; this could build resistance.

**8** Decide on the future direction of the enlarged organization and management strategies before any move is made.

**9** On acquiring another company, there may be parts that do not fit into future plans; have a policy for disposal.

**10** Decide in advance the financial limits.

CHECKLIST

# When not to merge or acquire

**1** When a review of the business shows that internal processes can be improved and that growth can be achieved internally.

**2** When the costs of either option would not be commensurate with the increased turnover and profits.

**3** When the cost of raising finance for an acquisition would not be covered by the sale of unwanted assets.

**4** When there is a danger of losing the identity of your company in either option.

**5** When there would be no chance of creating a working management structure for the enlarged business.

**6** When the market would not be able to support the planned increase in production.

**7** When the merger or acquisition would lead to the danger of a loss of intellectual property.

CHECKLIST

# 4

joint ventures and partnerships

# Reasons for collaboration

A joint venture is the pooling of resources and expertise by two or more businesses to achieve a particular goal. The risks and rewards are also shared.

There are various types of partnerships. Those that are most relevant to the idea of growing your business are discussed in this chapter.

The reasons for forming a partnership can vary according to the needs of the business, but the overall objective is to grow the business in a profitable way and to fill any gaps that might be holding the enterprise back.

It is vital to carry out an analysis of the business, prior to any collaboration, to see what areas of improvement can be identified. The SWOT analysis (pp. 26–27) is an ideal way to establish the compatibility of the proposed partner company to ensure that you make the most advantageous choices.

SOME OF THE MAIN REASONS DRIVING THESE DECISIONS CAN BE
SUMMARIZED AS FOLLOWS:

## 1 GAIN COMPETITIVE ADVANTAGE

The fewer companies that exist in the marketplace capable of
supplying to the same customers as you supply, the greater
the chance of increasing sales without diversifying into other
products and services. Through collaboration your company
can grow and at the same time reduce the amount of
competition you face.

## 2 SHARE RISKS

Business is all about taking risks. Ways to recognize where risk
lies in a business and the ways in which the risks can be
mitigated was described on pp. 38–45. Sharing risks, by
collaboration, is a good way to ease the burden of risk in your
own company.

# 100
**joint ventures and partnerships**
# Reasons for collaboration continued

**3** GAIN ACCESS TO MORE MARKETS AND CUSTOMERS
It will depend on the type of product or service that your
company can supply, but unless there is a certain amount of
obsolescence in the product, markets will eventually "dry up."
New markets have to be found, and this can prove to be an
expensive and time-consuming activity. Collaboration with
another company that has existing markets in other places,
perhaps overseas, is a way to increase your market share
without having to take the risks of new market penetration.

**4** GAIN ACCESS TO MORE KNOWLEDGE AND EXPERTISE
Keeping abreast of new technology, certainly in some fields of
expertise, involves setting up research and development
departments and investing a reasonable amount of retained
profit. Ensuring that your business is at the forefront of
progress will take a lot of time that will detract from the
normal day-to-day running. Collaboration with another
company that has a record of technological revolution is a
good way to benefit from their expertise and to maintain your
position in the market.

## 5 REDUCE COSTS AND LEAD-TIMES

One of the prime concerns in any business is to keep costs under control and, where possible, attempt to reduce costs without loss of quality or customer alienation. A major area of cost consumption is that concerned with the launch of a new product. As an example, look at the aerospace industry. To design, build, test, and prove a new aircraft is so costly that it is often beyond the reach of many of the world's leading companies, especially if the competition demands shortened lead-times to get the product operational. To overcome this problem, Airbus Industrie is a collaborative venture on the part of some of the large established aircraft constructors to pool resources and concentrate on certain aspects of aircraft construction to their mutual advantage.

# 102
**joint ventures and partnerships**
# Reasons for collaboration continued

**6** ACCELERATE THE RATE OF CHANGE
As someone once said, "constant change is here to stay" or "the only constant in today's changing world is change." A business cannot survive if it does not change to meet the prevailing conditions of choice and technology. Companies collaborate to ensure that they are not left behind in the race to provide what their customers want.

These reasons are very diverse in their aspirations, and so it is not surprising that many different types of collaboration have been developed by businesses to meet their own needs.

The types of collaboration to consider in the context of growth can range from the simple informal agreement through to the far more complicated equity joint venture agreement that creates a legal entity capable of trading in its own right.

THEY INCLUDE:

- Strategic collaborations
- Equity alliances
- Marketing collaborations
- Product and production collaborations
- Supply partnerships

# What is collaboration?

In a business context, the accepted definition of "collaboration" is to work with another on a joint project. Organizations work together for mutual advantage. Except in the case of an equity joint venture, there is rarely a major transfer of funds or a large investment of equity by one company in the other.

**1** The main requirements for any type of collaboration are trust, goodwill, and an expectation of mutual benefit.

**2** Although there is usually a firm contractual basis for all types of collaboration, trust is still an integral part of the success of the project.

**3** It is often necessary to protect some information, special skill, or process that does not become part of the transfer of information or that is not relevant to the project being jointly undertaken. This can and should be "ring-fenced," that is, funds are specifically set aside for use for this purpose and are used exclusively for it.

**4** If this protection is not provided, the business could suffer or even disappear. It is significant that this "fence" is understood by all of those people working on the project.

**5** It is natural for employees to want to show others their and their company's prowess and abilities and to "talk-up" the business to others. Ring-fencing is vital.

**6** This can result in the disclosure of company confidential information that is both necessary for the advancement of technology and for market position.

# Which type of collaboration?

Although several types of collaboration are described in the following pages, there are no hard and fast rules that can be applied to determine the most advantageous type of collaboration for your business.

**1** A great deal depends on the circumstances and reasons behind the strategy that you select as the most likely to meet the needs of the partner companies.

**2** It will be necessary to tailor the detail of the partnership to suit an individual business.

**3** Often businesses find it appropriate to mix and match different types of collaboration.

**4** It is often the case that the mix changes during the lifetime of the partnership.

**5** If there are several partners in the project, then it is normal to have a different type of agreement with each one.

**6** Although the flexibility of joint ventures, and collaborations in general, should be mentioned, it is also pertinent to explain that such amalgamations of companies do not need to be a lifetime commitment.

**7** Many joint ventures are formed for a limited lifespan, to further a specific project and, on the completion of the task, are disbanded.

**joint ventures and partnerships**

# Strategic alliance

The terms "strategic alliance" and "joint venture" are interchangeable. A strategic alliance is often set up when a separate legal entity is not required.

**1** The idea of a strategic alliance is for two or more companies to pool ideas and resources to work on a common item.

**2** There is no amalgamation of the companies, and neither of them loses any part of their identity.

**3** At the end of the agreement, they will continue to trade as they have always done.

**4** This form of alliance could lead into a more formal agreement.

As an example, the car manufacturers Volkswagen, SEAT, and Ford entered into a strategic alliance for the development of a new MPV (multi-purpose vehicle) product range. Each company adopted the basic design, but each added its own special touches to customize the finished vehicles to its own specifications. This eventually led to a new manufacturing facility under the name AutoEuropa that was based in Portugal.

The terms of the strategic alliance are agreed at the outset and will cover areas such as:

- Extent of the work
- Time scales
- Information sharing
- Termination
- Cost sharing
- Risk sharing
- Ownership of intellectual property rights
- Use of information generated by the project

## Strategic alliance continued

**1** A strategic alliance can be the preliminary step to forming a joint venture agreement that will create a separate company trading in its own right. ☐

**2** It allows companies to work together to achieve a stated objective common to both partners. ☐

**3** Partners maintain their independence throughout the period of the alliance. ☐

**4** Airline companies often form a strategic alliance: On certain routes an alliance allows ticketing, check-in facilities, and baggage handling to be done by either airline. ☐

**5** British Airways and Iberia operate a strategic alliance on routes between London and Spanish cities. ☐

**6** Ford, Volkswagen, and SEAT had a strategic alliance for the design and development of the MPV (multi-purpose vehicle) that was manufactured by AutoEuropa in Portugal. The products were badged as Galaxy and Alhambra. ☐

**7** The alliance can be dissolved once the strategic objective has been reached. ☐

**CHECKLIST**

# Strategic partnership

This differs from the strategic alliance in that one of the partners usually takes a minority financial stake in the other company, but not enough to form an acquisition or takeover.

**1** A separate business entity is not formed.

**2** The partnership is formed to strengthen or fill a weakness or gap in the operational ability of one of the partners.

**3** As an example, consider that your business may produce items of excellent quality but that finding the right markets and outlets is proving difficult.

**4** Partnering with a company that has the necessary expertise in finding such markets will be to mutual advantage.

**5** It could be that the reverse is the case: You have the ability to access these markets and are seeking further products to extend your range, but you do not want the expense of new development and production.

**6** Having a financial stake in the other business is a good way to bind the enterprises closer together.

# 114
**joint ventures and partnerships**
## Strategic partnership continued

**7** This method is frequently applied in the Japanese automotive component supply industry as part of the "Keiretsu" process where the car manufacturer provides some equity to the supplier. This may be for a nominated purpose such as investment in new research or provision of new tooling.

**8** Airlines also use strategic partnerships. They buy minority equity stakes in competitor and feeder airlines so that "code sharing" in ticket sales can occur.

**9** It also enables them to offer "through ticketing" to destinations that they do not serve but are served by their partner airline.

**10** This improves customer loyalty. Some of these partnerships are so strong that the smaller partners often adopt the same livery of aircraft and uniforms and share airport facilities and check-in arrangements.

**joint ventures and partnerships**

# Strategic partnership continued

Strategic partnerships are particularly useful when two companies want to bring their complementary skills and abilities together to offer a combined package to a customer.

**1** It fits in with a planned growth. ☐

**2** It allows two high-profile companies to collaborate for mutual advantage. ☐

**3** No separate entity is created as the partnership only operates when one of the companies receives an enquiry from an outside source for the service that they both provide. ☐

**4** One of the major benefits is that the two companies get to know each other well, which will improve their working relationships. ☐

A classic example of working in this way is a telecommunications service provider who develops strategic partnerships with various companies to offer communication-based solutions to business needs.

**CHECKLIST**

# Joint venture company (JVC)

There is no universally recognized definition of a joint venture.

**1** The most common definition is a collaborative business venture, formed by two or more separate organizations for a particular purpose and that creates an "independent business entity" for that purpose.

**2** A JVC allocates ownership, operational responsibilities, and financial risks and rewards to each member while preserving their separate identities and autonomy.

**3** The majority of joint venture companies are so-called equity JVCs. They are formed by the input of various forms of equity by the business organizations that make up the parent companies.

**4** The equity can take various forms but usually consists of cash investment, technology investment, plant, machinery, land, buildings, and even management skills.

**5** The JVC has its own identity and will be a legal entity, able to trade and carry on the business for which it was formed.

**6** The rewards (both profits and losses) are allocated between the partner companies, usually in a direct ratio to the equity allocated. Equity allocation can be determined either at the start-up phase or as a result of further modifications during the course of the agreement.

**7** JVCs can be formed for a number of purposes covering such diverse functions as design and development, production, technology transfer, and marketing. It is not unusual for companies in direct competition with each other to set up a JVC and to remain in competition during the lifetime of the JVC.

**8** If the two companies are in competition, it is necessary to set clear boundaries when the JVC is formed, detailing what the JVC can do so that neither founding company is compromised.

**9** Clearly define an "end point" at the start unless it is intended that at some future date the JVC should be restructured and perhaps floated off as a separate and self-contained business, no longer dependent upon nor answerable to either of the establishing organizations.

International joint ventures are becoming increasingly popular as a way for businesses to break into new and developing markets overseas and for the transfer of technology into developing companies to help to build up indigenous manufacture.

**1** One of numerous examples of this type of JVC include the sale of automotive technology and the means of manufacture to the burgeoning Chinese motor vehicle industry.

**2** In such cases an end point is not always feasible and the joint venture should continue to operate as long as it conforms to normal business criteria.

**3** Some of the pitfalls that could be encountered in international joint ventures are the ratio of the equity holding (government restrictions on the level of foreign investment) and the repatriation of profits from the country in which the JVC is established.

**4** It is also the case that intellectual property right protection is not observed as strictly as it should be in some countries.

# Joint venture company (JVC) continued

Sales of finished products from the JVC need to be considered.

**1** Depending on the type of JVC established, the output might be sold back to the partner companies for them to sell on to their customers.

**2** A direct marketing system could be set up allowing the JVC to sell direct to customers within certain designated markets and territories.

Diagrammatic examples of joint venture companies are shown opposite and on p. 125. This example shows the specific nature of a JVC.

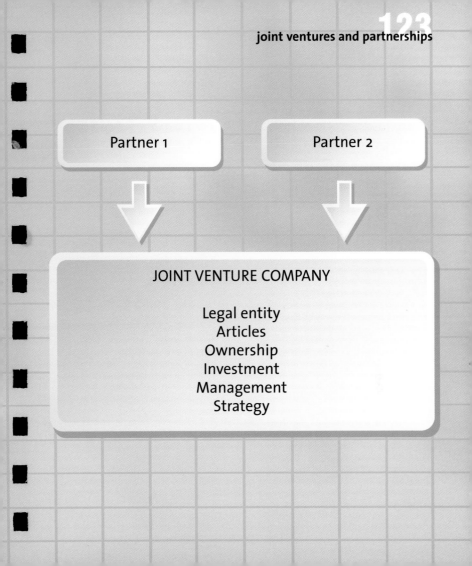

# Joint venture company (JVC) continued

This second diagram shows the possible equity items that each partner company might provide to the joint venture.

**1** If partner 1 supplies components or finished products to the JVC, then royalties could be paid.

**2** If partner 2 made facilities available, certainly in the case of land and/or buildings, then rent for these facilities could be paid from the JVC.

The contractual arrangements involved in the formation of a joint venture company are complex and are best handled by a specialist legal firm. Imprecise agreements can lead to a possible breakdown of the JVC, and that would be a costly exercise to put right.

**PRODUCT AND PRODUCTION COLLABORATIONS**
These are other forms of collaboration that enable a business to grow by using the technology and technical expertise of other companies to enhance its own abilities without incurring the expense of major investment into research and development and production facilities.

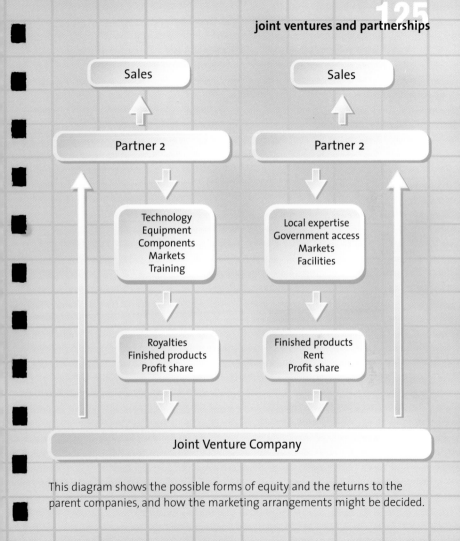

This diagram shows the possible forms of equity and the returns to the parent companies, and how the marketing arrangements might be decided.

# Joint venture company (JVC) continued

Joint ventures are a way of allowing resources and expertise to be shared to achieve a particular aim. Use this checklist to determine whether a JVC is right for your business.

**1** Do you want to expand into new products? ☐

**2** Do you want to expand into new markets? ☐

**3** Do you want to expand but lack the resources for a dedicated R & D policy? ☐

**4** Do you want to expand but lack the resources to undertake marketing in new areas? ☐

**5** Do you need more resources? ☐

**6** Do you need increased capacity? ☐

**7** Do you want to expand into markets in other parts of the world? ☐

**8** Are you happy to share risks so that the whole burden is not placed on your company? ☐

CHECKLIST

# Research and design collaboration

There are now specialist research and design companies that will undertake work on your behalf and apply the brainpower of their own resources on behalf of your problems and ideas.

**1** They have one or two experts in your type of business who understand the environment in which you work and can apply that knowledge to your advantage.

**2** One of the key issues to be managed in this type of collaboration involves the ownership of the new ideas, products, and processes generated in the collaboration.

**3** The major sources of this type of collaboration are universities where graduate research engineers, for example, equipped with the state-of-the-art facilities, are able to offer solutions to your problem and, in many cases, can show examples of the proposed solutions. This is particularly relevant when the solution is sufficiently novel to justify it being protected by a patent or copyright.

**4** Ownership of these rights is extremely important, as they form a valuable part of a business's intangible assets.

**5** All rules covering the ownership of intellectual property must be established at the start of the agreement.

**6** The normal rule is that the party who pays for the work to be carried out owns the rights to such property; however, the subject can be clouded by legal arguments as to questions of "background" and "foreground" information.

**7** It is vital to established who brought what knowledge to the research (background information) and who created the new knowledge (foreground information).

**joint ventures and partnerships**

# Joint production

Joint production is a form of collaboration in which two or more companies collaborate to produce separate parts of a complete product and support one of the partners to carry out the final assembly operation.

**1** This type of collaboration differs from the normal customer/supplier partnership in that partners share equally in the risks and rewards.

**2** The new Airbus A380 aircraft is an example of joint production. The main parts of the airplane (wings, fuselage, engines) are produced by different companies with the final assembly being undertaken in a different facility.

**3** The disadvantage of this type of collaboration can be the technical and logistical complexity involved.

**4** The great advantage of this type of collaboration is that it allows the individual companies to remain in as separate production entities and still achieve growth.

# Licensing

There are times when you want to expand your business to take advantage of new markets and/or new customers.

**1** The opportunity may present itself to widen the horizons of sales to overseas markets in which you know you could succeed and that would prove to be profitable.

**2** The opportunity is there, waiting for you to take advantage of the situation.

**3** You are unable to increase your production sufficiently to supply in both markets.

**4**  You may not have the facilities to cope.

**5**  You may not have the workforce to meet production targets.

**6**  Lack of finance may prevent you from taking full advantage of the situation.

**7**  One possibility is to enter into a licensing arrangement with another company, perhaps but not necessarily in the vicinity of the possible market.

# Licensing continued

A licensing agreement is a formal agreement between businesses in which the primary company gives official permission to another to manufacture and/or trade its proprietary products, or copy its services and "know-how" in the marketplace.

**1** Such licenses are legally binding and generally involve the payment of fees to cover the supply of initial information such as design, manufacturing, and processing to enable the product to be identical in all respects.

**2** You may also wish to grant the use of patented information and to allow the secondary company to use the product name and trademark to enhance product value or customer acceptance of the product or services or both.

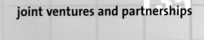

**3** Product names and trademarks need to be protected under the agreement.

**4** It is also necessary to oversee and approve the quality of the finished product or service to ensure that the good name of your company is not harmed.

**5** To recompense for the loss of profit encountered because the manufacture and sale has occurred in another place, you should request a royalty payment for each item sold.

# Licensing continued

**6** A royalty could be a fixed amount or a percentage of the selling price. You should negotiate what this will be at the agreement stage.

**7** Royalties can remain constant throughout the life of the agreement or can be linked to the amount of products sold.

**8** The license can be for a fixed period of time or unlimited.

**9** The license can be exclusive to the licensee or applicable only for specified markets.

**10** Another strategy is to buy back some of the finished products to sell in your markets, thereby increasing your sales potential without the need for more internal facilities.

**11** It is a normal part of the growth strategy to "license-in" products that you could manufacture and sell to your own customers and thereby diversify without the risk of developing a new product that might not be accepted by your existing customers.

```
┌─────────────────────────────────────┐
│              Licensor               │
└─────────────────────────────────────┘
        ↓                    ↓
┌──────────────────┐  ┌──────────────────┐
│    Royalties     │  │    Technology    │
│ Lump sum payments│  │Technical assistance│
│Component revenues│  │    Equipment     │
│ Finished products│  │    components    │
└──────────────────┘  └──────────────────┘
        ↓                    ↓
┌─────────────────────────────────────┐
│              Licensee               │
└─────────────────────────────────────┘
```

This example shows how a license agreement might work.

joint ventures and partnerships
# Franchising

One growth strategy that ensures that the integrity of your product is maintained is a franchise agreement.

**1** A franchise agreement allows a manufacturer to permit a distributor to market the manufacturer's products.

**2** It can also be used to cover the provision of services.

**3** The primary company can appoint secondary companies as "franchised" dealers or agents for its products or services.

**4** Motor manufacturers, for example, franchise dealers to sell their products exclusively in certain geographical areas.

**5** Other examples are fast food outlets, photo processing, and dry-cleaning establishments.

**6** The primary company's name and logo figure exclusively on the premises, and the primary company supplies the constituent parts of the product with strict specifications as to use and presentation.

**7** With a franchise agreement, the marketing risks are borne by the secondary company, although usually the primary company approves the siting of the outlet.

**8** Some multiple product shops franchise the selling, usually of luxury products by a number of independent franchises of specific product lines (such as a particular brand of fashion items or perfumes).

**joint ventures and partnerships**

# Choosing franchising over licensing

As a general rule, franchising is done to allow a product or service to be marketed by a franchisee in accordance with strict guidelines imposed by the franchisor.

**1** Franchising is sometimes confused with licensing as the term is often used in both cases.

**2** A franchisee is allowed to trade under the trademark or trade name of the franchisor.

**3** With a franchise, the franchisor supplies all the elements necessary to establish a business that can be run by an individual or team without previous experience of the product or business.

**4** A business can choose to grow not by developing new products or finding new markets but by allowing others to sell a product or service.

**5** A license is usually granted to another company with a proven track record in similar products to manufacture and sell goods, either back to the licensor or into those markets specified by the licensor.

**6** A franchise is regarded as a long-term undertaking, whereas a license is normally for a short or medium term.

# Supply partnerships

Over the past decade, there has been a rapid development of partnerships with suppliers of components, facilities, and services.

**1** A supply company is heavily dependent on the purchaser for its own success and vice versa.

**2** This reality is becoming increasingly recognized by US and European businesses that, in the past, have tended to keep their suppliers at arm's length and deal with them in a confrontational manner.

**3** Many manufacturers now admit to sourcing 60 percent of their total sales revenue from their suppliers.

**4** These purchased items, when assembled into the finished product, have a critical effect on the appearance, performance, and functionality of the products.

**5** To ensure consistent supply and to maintain customer confidence, it is essential that good teamwork exists between all partners within the "supply chain."

**6** It has been the custom for manufacturers to show their strength in negotiation by attempting to beat down the supplier on price and to change suppliers if they are offered cheaper components.

**7** Such a practice offers a short-term cost advantage but may have harmful long-term consequences.

# Supply partnerships continued

Some companies, many of them Japanese, have developed a different approach to the supplier/customer relationship.

**1** They have recognized the importance of the supplier in the consistency of their products and seen excellent partnership arrangements as a major part of their business strategy.

**2** Their view is that the supplier should be considered as an extension of their own enterprise and treated accordingly.

**3** They have made their suppliers aware of the order book situation and have arranged, through their financial and banking associates, acceptable long-term finance to enable growth through investment.

**4** By this means, they have been able to eliminate duplication and wasteful practices, thereby improving quality and reducing cost and lead-times.

**5** Some elements of the Japanese approach would not be acceptable under American and European law due to local rulings on competition.

**6** However, the benefits that arise from joint involvement and mutual trust, just-in-time supply, and Total Quality Management are now considered to be worth exploiting by a growing number of companies.

# Supply partnerships continued

There are several steps to making your joint venture relationship work.

**1** Make sure the agreement is well prepared, unambiguous, and acceptable to all partners.

**2** A major part of building a good relationship is communication. Schedule regular meetings with key people involved in the joint venture to ensure that people know what is involved and what progress has been made.

**3** Try to identify problems at an early stage and do not play the "blame game."

**4** Set clear objectives from the outset and monitor progress. Measure performance by clear performance indicators.

**5** Share information especially in the more sensitive areas such as finance. This helps to dispel mistrust.

**6** Try to establish achievable goals and ensure everyone works toward them, but at the same time allow for some flexibility and have a provision for changing your objectives if need be.

# 5

benefits and risks
of collaboration

# Risks vs. benefits

There are risks and benefits involved In all types of collaboration, and your business strategy should be to maximize the benefits and to minimize the risks. In order to do this, you must first identify them. Paradoxically, it can be that a benefit may also be a risk, but this is usually so when viewed from the perspective of a different party.

The following pages list risks and benefits in no particular order of priority. The weight given to each benefit or risk is dependent on the reasons for the chosen collaboration in the first place. A factor that might be a major priority for one company could be of little significance for another. What is important is that each partner in the collaboration sees the possibility of mutual benefit that will give a competitive advantage to each of them over their own competitors in the marketplace.

The skill in developing a partnership is knowing when to start and, just as importantly, when to terminate it. Reviewing the actual progress and comparing this to the hoped-for benefits is important, since that is the only way to assess the actual benefits, or identify the unplanned risks and know when to stop the operation. This should happen before the risks are clearly starting to outweigh the benefits.

# Benefits of collaboration

**1** IMPROVE BUYING POWER

Improved buying power is also known as economies of scale as the combined needs of both partners should produce some form of leverage when buying from one supplier.

It can also reduce playing off by suppliers that occurs when companies are in competition to buy from a supplier a specific item that could be in short supply. This is a dangerous maneuver if the supplier can prove in law that this could be regarded as a restrictive practice or that the partners were forming a cartel.

**2** SHARE "AFTER MARKET" SUPPORT COSTS

With, for example, domestic appliances becoming increasingly complex, specialist maintenance facilities are necessary for repair. It is possible for small repair businesses to collaborate to undertake repair and maintenance tasks for several manufacturers. A similar collaboration also applies to automotive repair organizations.

## 3 FILL GAP IN RESOURCES

This is a very frequent cause for collaborations for several reasons. A company undergoing rapid growth may not be able to expand all its in-house processes at the same speed to meet the demand and may need to take on partners to provide extra capacity. Similarly, a company finding that it has gaps in its coverage of the marketplace may take on partners who have the capability of solving the problem. Gaps frequently open up when product and process technology changes or new legislation is introduced that eliminates current processes and forces the introduction of new ones.

The rapid rate of change in IT, CAD CAM, e-commerce, environmental legislation, product miniaturization, the introduction of new materials, and manufacturing processes frequently leaves companies exposed to gaps in people and process capability. Recruitment, training, and refacilitation can fill these gaps, but this can be time-consuming (it takes an average 2–5 years). The alternative is to seek partners who already have the necessary skills and processes available.

# Benefits of collaboration continued

**4** CREATE LARGER POOL OF RESOURCES

The Italian company Olivetti is an excellent example of using collaboration/alliances to access a larger pool of resources. In an expensive advertising program in the early 1990s, it claimed that it had set up alliances with 229 "leading edge" companies around the world, and by this process it was able to expand its R & D capability to bring in over 3500 scientists and engineers, to assist develop its new products. This is far more than the number of staff it could afford to support on its own R & D payroll, and represented a very successful "leveraging" of a scarce resource.

**5** SHARE RESEARCH AND DEVELOPMENT COSTS

If a company tries to enter a new field of business, or progress in its current field too quickly, it will be unable to fund the high cost of the research and development. It could be possible to enter the market more quickly by partnering with another company that has already developed the product. This is often the reason for collaborations between partners in different parts of the world.

# 6 IMPROVE MORALE IF HANDLED WELL

The "feel-good factor" can be engendered among the employees of a company when a partnership or license deal is set up with a successful partner who is widely recognized as the market leader in some area of business.

Producers of Coca-Cola and Pepsi soft drinks outside the USA are generally not companies wholly owned by the brand copyright holder—other companies have obtained a license or formed a joint venture company to produce and sell these products in different markets. Because of the excellent brand image of the products, the licensees generally succeed in business. However, they must perform to the strict "letter of the license" to retain the rights to use, and the benefits accruing from, the brands.

# Benefits of collaboration continued

**7**   TAKE ADVANTAGE OF SPECIALIZATION OPPORTUNITIES

Producers of electronic products rarely design and manufacture all the complex components in their products. They will generally set up supply arrangements with specialist component producers for their microchips and many other components. Some of this procurement is achieved by simple purchase contracts, but more and more it is becoming the practice to establish long-term "preferred suppliers," "evergreen contracts," or "Kieretsu" relationships. Under these arrangements, the supplier is seen as an "extended part of the enterprise," in genuine partnership with the business customer for the foreseeable future.

Another form of specialization opportunity is in the area of meeting particular business needs. For example, most big companies in the past have employed their own in-house systems developers, IT specialists, security, catering, and other non-core activity staff. Most companies are now realizing that these can be run more effectively and cheaply by calling in specialist companies to replace in-house people and facilities. The specialist partners that they choose are experts in the particular field, whose very business survival depends on their being at least one step ahead of the competition.

**8** OPEN NEW MARKETS

It is essential for any company of any country that is trying to develop new markets to find a partner in virtually every new market it wishes to enter. Rolls-Royce aero engines and VW cars are typical large Western companies that are doing very good business in China through joint ventures with local partners, and British Airways is seeking to add new partnerships to extend its networks.

**158**
**benefits and risks of collaboration**
# Benefits of collaboration continued

**9** ACCESS "RESTRICTED" MARKETS
The new markets of the world—China, Malaysia, India, and other Pacific Rim countries—are undergoing rapid economic growth. These countries may, in difficult economic conditions, impose restrictions on movement of currency to protect their foreign exchange balance. This happened in Malaysia in 1998. As part of this economic management process, countries may also impose various restrictions on how business can be conducted. These restrictions often make it essential to join with a local partner, if only to be able to understand all the subtleties of local requirements. Without such a partner, you may not be able to access these markets at all.

Many countries still have strict limits on foreign equity holdings and rates of indigenization and often look for "countertrade" and offsets to balance the outflow and inflow of foreign exchange.

**10** PROVIDE GREATER INFLUENCE ON MARKET AND REGULATIONS
Companies can join forces in many ways to influence their
hold on the market. They may join together in marketing
agreements, join their businesses together in loose
collaborations, form strategic partnerships or joint venture
companies, or carry out full mergers or acquisitions of each
other's businesses. The main purpose of these partnerships is
to strengthen the partners' hold on the market and to reduce
or even block competition.

There is a limit to such partnerships, particularly at the
mergers and acquisitions end of the scale. These tend to be
strictly policed by various government agencies in the USA.
The intention is to prevent any grouping of companies from
dominating the market against the consumer's interest.

## Benefits of collaboration continued

**11** ACCESS BETTER METHODS AND PROCESSES
Japan has developed "world best practice" standards in production and purchasing, and many US and European companies have gathered evidence of the benefits of applying some of the Japanese methods. These include just-in-time stock management, reduced layers of management, "empowered" production operatives, supplier partnerships, "Geba Ka" problem-solving techniques, and parts-per-million quality processes.

Companies that have collaborated with Japanese partners have had first-hand experience of these methods and have found them beneficial to growth.

## 12 INCREASE FINANCIAL RESOURCES AND STABILITY

All the partners in any project contribute their financial strength in appropriate ways to the joint operations. This itself increases the financial stability for all the businesses, increasing the power to borrow capital to fund new products and facilities. This process of borrowing capital funds brings financial institutions such as banks more closely into partnership with manufacturers (although often the short-term view taken by banks can itself be a major risk to the business partners).

Financing houses increase their involvement in business by loan rescheduling and "lease-back" arrangements. By this means, the banks own the machines and facilities that the manufacturing businesses use and are reimbursed with both capital and interest to a set formula over a specified period of time, after which the machines in question revert back to the ownership of the production business. A further refinement is that large companies frequently mastermind and arrange partnerships between their suppliers, who need funds for new equipment and tooling, and suitable financing institutions that will provide the loans, in a three-way arrangement that gives a greater feeling of security to all parties.

# Benefits of collaboration continued

## 13 BUILD A DEFENSIVE WALL

One of the excesses of Western business has been its passion for acquisitions, mergers, and takeovers. This was particularly true in the late 1990s and early 2000s in the scramble for globalization among the major companies, as witnessed in pharmaceuticals, communications, automotive, and other major industries (Glaxo Smith Kline, Vodafone AirTouch Mannesmann, DaimlerChrysler, for example).

For a business to stay independent of such tactics, it must be constantly vigilant of predator companies and "corporate raiders." It must find ways, therefore, of setting up defensive walls or find itself possibly facing very expensive actions to fight off such raiders. It is not unknown for companies to be forced to spend very large sums of money to keep their independence in the face of hostile takeovers. This results in no "added value" to the business, and may have serious adverse effects on their continuing operation.

The Japanese automotive industry has created a most effective "defensive wall" strategy by grouping its business customers in partnership with their suppliers, in clusters called Kieretsus.

This process often involves an equity exchange with some form of "golden share" arrangement. The value of the golden share is unique and unquantifiable. In essence, it has the power to prevent any predator from buying a supplier without the agreement of the other partners.

In Japan, this agreement is rarely given, as Japanese companies have worked extremely hard on their supply partners to form an extended family grouping of companies all working in a like-minded partnership. All the companies in a Kieretsu have the same objective—the success of each other in business. They believe that secure long-term partnerships offer the most effective means of achieving this success.

This technique is not acceptable in many territories, but an equivalent "next best" approach is to form mature supply partnerships without equity interchange.

# Benefits of collaboration continued

## 14 PURSUE AN AGGRESSIVE STRATEGY

Once a defensive wall strategy is in place, it provides the ideal platform for an aggressive growth strategy. A company with strong partners in each of its marketplaces, and strong partnerships with all its suppliers, is clearly in better shape than unpartnered competitors to provide its customers with new good-quality products at an advantageous price quickly.

This partnership process was at the heart of the growth and success over the last 30–40 years of the Japanese industrial machine. To keep pace and improve on Japanese business performance, other industrial nations found their own versions of collaboration and partnership strategies (which comply with national legislation) to give them a unique competitive advantage.

## 15 BENEFIT FROM SYNERGY

The equation 1 + 1 = more than 2 has frequently proved to be true in the context of business partnerships. Two companies pooling their knowledge, skills, and resources often cause each other to produce better ideas than each on their own would achieve. Clubs of several companies working together should be able to do even better. This is one of the main reasons for the formation of government-funded multicompany, multination, multiacademia partnerships. Success to date proves that synergy occurs in such situations when partnerships are well-managed.

# Risks of collaboration

It would be unrealistic to discuss the benefits of partnerships, without identifying that there are the possibilities of major risks.

## 1 LOSE OVERALL CONTROL OF PARTNERSHIP PROJECT, OR STEAMROLLERING

The stronger partner in a collaboration program is likely to dictate the pace and specification of work to be carried out. In other words, one partner may impose, or "steamroller" their views over the objections of the others. If this is causing distress to the partnership, the only realistic course of action is to pull out and seek another way to achieve your objectives.

The essence of collaboration and partnerships is that companies work wholeheartedly together. Reaching for the contract agreement and inviting the lawyers to quote the small print at each other is a clear sign that the partnership will serve no further useful purpose unless it is totally renegotiated. Lawyers' fees are expensive, litigation in court is hugely costly, and the outcome is unpredictable as it depends on the quality of the lawyers and their skill in guiding the judge and jury to find in favor of one party or another.

## 2 LOSE IDENTITY

Individual collaborating companies may well lose their identity in partnership programs. This needs to be recognized and planned for from the start.

For example, the collaboration between British Aerospace, Aerospatiale (France), DASA (Germany), and Casa (Spain) to produce the Airbus range of commercial aircraft does not reflect the names of any of the partner companies in this "joint production" program. Old customer loyalty may be lost as a result of this; however, a well-managed partnership will soon create new customer loyalty.

## Risks of collaboration continued

**3** LOSE COMPANY THROUGH TROJAN HORSE, OR FAILURE OF PARTNER
In setting up collaborative projects, care must be taken to ensure that each partner understands the other's long-term objective. Many partnerships are deliberately set up to give one side more advantage than the other. Most emerging businesses wish to extract from their maturer partner as much knowledge, skill, expertise, and company secrets as possible, with the long-term view of taking over the total business. This is described as the Trojan Horse principle. It is a normal business process, which must be recognized and planned for by the mature partner, who has to place clear boundaries around any partnership project, and define "no go" areas that must be clearly communicated to its partners and, most importantly, to its own employees.

Governments of developing countries encourage this process of technology transfer, usually by demanding a progressive transfer of manufacturing and design capability into their own marketplace. This indigenization program is identified to the external partner at the time of obtaining permits and licenses to start the project. A typical program may be 10 percent local content in year 1 of production, 20 percent in year 2, 40 percent in year 3, and 60–80 percent in year 5. By year 5, control of the project may be lost by the mature partner and, unless well-managed, may even lead to its being wiped out. Companies wishing to trade in countries with such rules must be aware of and plan for the risk. Promises of indigenization, which later are not delivered, can have serious consequences and may lead to litigation for breach of contract and/or the withdrawal of government approval and licenses to continue in business.

# Risks of collaboration continued

**4** LEAVE "HOLES" IN PROJECTS
Poor selection of partners may cause serious problems if they fail to deliver their part of the deal. Careful vetting of all prospective partners is clearly an essential part of successful management.

**5** EXPOSE CONFIDENTIALITY ISSUES
Maintaining company secrets is a problem for all businesses, especially when new products, processes, and technology are concerned. The problems are to some extent more difficult when working in collaboration with others. Each partner, as a precondition of the work being developed together, should sign confidentiality agreements. Where new developments are contemplated, these agreements must define how the new intellectual property right is to be apportioned between the partners and, at the commercial exploitation stage, how the rewards will be shared. Breach of confidentiality may be a just cause for termination of the partnership and lead to legal action for damages.

**6** ENGAGE IN COMMUNICATION AND TRANSLATION PROBLEMS
The more obvious language difficulties in multinational projects can be greatly increased if the meaning behind the spoken word is misunderstood. As a very simple example, it is difficult for a Japanese businessman to say "no," and he will frequently say "yes" when "no" is what he means. The "yes," or the positive shake of the head, may simply mean that he has heard your question or point of view. You must repeat the question in another way, or even several different ways, to be sure that "yes" actually means "yes."

Literal translation of another language can be extremely dangerous, as the result is frequently misleading and often gibberish. Always have two translators, your own who speaks the foreign language and the other company's translator who speaks yours. The correct story will emerge somewhere between the two.

# Risks of collaboration continued

**7** WORK WITH DIFFERENT STANDARDS AND PROCEDURES
Though British, Chinese, American, or Indian companies are
accustomed to using their own national standards and
procedures, such as work measurement and machine
efficiency, which generally are at the heart of costing a project,
they do not easily understand that these differ from country
to country.

The EU is beginning to achieve common standards for many
things such as quality, measurement of quantities, and work
standards and are migrating toward an International ISO
series of standards, but there is still room for considerable
misunderstandings. USA uses a mixture of imperial and metric
units, and even different volumetric measures for the gallon.

Some of these potential problems are quite obvious and can be easily dealt with. More invidious are differences in interpretation of nominally the same thing, like standard minutes of labor, which can vary from company to company and country to country. Major blunders in contract costing can result from these issues, making the difference between profit and loss. Once again the only answer is to manage the problem by doing the necessary research beforehand, and correcting for known discrepancies as they arise.

The areas of risk include costing, technical standards and measures, legal processes, environmental requirements, health and safety aspects, financial regulations, and transportation.

# Risks of collaboration continued

**8**  LOSE IN-HOUSE SKILLS/EXPERTISE
The concern most frequently expressed is that by giving up some element of your own business expertise to put it in the hands of a specialist partner, your company will eventually not be expert enough to stand alone in the event of the eclipse of the partner. Also, internal managers worry that when their in-house expertise disappears, the specialist suppliers will somehow exploit the situation.

This must be examined against the fact that for most manufacturing and utilities companies, some 50–80 percent of their business is totally dependent on their many suppliers, most of whom are respectable and honorable.

The benefits from partnerships are too great to allow a few bad partners to discolor the whole picture. Once again, the solution comes from being aware of the potential problem and managing the process to eliminate the risk.

Once in-house skill has gone, it is difficult and time-consuming to recreate it. But to double-guess, or double-engineer your partner's expertise is expensive, and poses an even bigger threat to the business. Supply partnerships based on mutual trust, mutual benefit, and "open book trading" are clearly the best way of minimizing this risk.

# Risks of collaboration continued

**9** LOSE TECHNOLOGY KNOW-HOW LEADERSHIP
Clearly, no business would want to give away its leadership in areas of its core skills and the expertise that distinguishes it from other companies. On the other hand, the exposure of its business heartland to partners can result in a gradual or even rapid leaking away of the core.

The best way to minimize this risk is to develop long-term partnerships in which the zones of core skills are identified clearly for each partner and "boundaries" are set and agreed. These boundaries in general should only be revisited when some major change such as new technology impacts on the business interface. This is not an easy task to achieve if your own business environment is not used to this type of process.

**10** DEAL WITH DEMANDS FOR EXTRA PRIORITY AND VIGILANCE
Companies that are not familiar with collaboration and
partnership strategies must take great care in adopting these
ideas and implementing them. Selection of partners cannot be
left to inexperienced managers. It is a difficult and demanding
process to do all the necessary "up front" research and
planning, and it must be done thoroughly.

By creating partnerships, you are trying to operate as a closely
integrated business, but without the benefit of strong equity
links in the form of vertical integration. To set this up requires
your most widely experienced managers, if a naïve and
dangerous result is to be avoided. Once the process is up and
running, it still needs your best managers, that is, the ones
who can find solutions to problems as they occur rather than
run immediately to the contract and subsequent litigation.

It is vital to ascertain any hidden agenda that may exist
behind the subjects under discussion. A Trojan Horse take-over
may be the partner's hidden objective. Only in-depth research
and good managers can minimize this type of risk. You do not
want to implement a plan that makes lawyers wealthy, at the
expense of your business.

# Risks of collaboration continued

**11** RECOGNIZE CULTURAL DIFFERENCES
There is no shortcut to dealing with this issue. The partners must carry out intensive research into the do's and don'ts of the respective national and company cultures and make considerable efforts to respect them. In international projects, it is essential to have a collaborative partner who is local to the situations and can guide you through this potential minefield. Never send executives who are untrained in these issues to negotiate or manage projects in countries of a significantly different culture. With a single unknowing discourteous action, they can destroy all the work done and the goodwill that engenders mutual trust.

**12 ENCOUNTER ADVERSE REACTION OF EMPLOYEES AND TRADE UNIONS**
The question that sometimes comes from shop floor
employees and union representatives is "Why have you given
all this work away to your partners?" Careful communication
and explanation of the reasons behind your plans is the best
way to minimize the risk of demotivating your own people or
causing potentially serious industrial relations problems.

# Risks of collaboration continued

## 13 GET INVOLVED IN MONOPOLIES AND MERGERS ISSUES

In Europe, companies must operate under the influence of EU Directives, which limit the size and scope of some partnership ambitions. Partnerships that are formed without the involvement of equity ownership tend to be freer of control from EU commissioners, on the presumption that they do not contravene any directives or laws.

It is interesting to note that one of the fastest growing business management processes in the USA for the purpose of improving business performance is the formation of strategic alliances, or nonequity partnerships.

## 14 ASSUME ACCOUNTABILITY FOR FAILURE

In the business world, there is usually a "witch hunt" to find the people who caused any failure, and failures of collaborations are no exception. Because partners, by definition, share responsibility in one way or another, it is frequently more difficult to find the guilty parties. Each tends to blame the other for the disaster. To prevent this, there must be a clear project specification and statement of "who does what, with which, to whom, and by when." This is a normal project management requirement for any program.

# Risks of collaboration continued

## 15 KEEP ON TOP OF DIVERGING COMPANY STRATEGIES

Business is a dynamic process subjected to continual change due to predictable and unpredictable circumstances. It is important that all business relationships, such as collaborations, which are not cemented by at least a majority stakeholding, should be under frequent review to ensure that the prevailing circumstances that caused them to be set up are still relevant at some future date.

Clearly defined contracts are a means of creating stability but are of little or no use if the surrounding circumstances change significantly. Collaboration agreements should recognize this reality and have clear statements about what can bring a partnership to an end. This should be planned for at the start of a partnership and included in any subsequent written agreement or contract.

## 16 RECOGNIZE CURRENCY FLUCTUATIONS AND TAKE ON THE COST OF PROTECTION

One of the biggest risks to any form of international trade is the volatility of the financial markets. Movements between the yen, yuan, dollar, euro, pound, rouble, rupee, and other currencies are unpredictable at best and troubled by international currency speculation at worst.

To achieve some degree of protection of the value of oil transactions in the Western world, all business is conducted in US dollars.

Most currency protection processes themselves cost money, as someone else such as a bank takes on the inherent risk. If you wish to be in international business, you must plan for and manage this risk, using all the financial management processes available to companies operating in your sector of the market.

# 184
**benefits and risks of collaboration**
## Risks of collaboration continued

**17** DEAL WITH INADEQUATE/BAD CONTRACTUAL AGREEMENTS
Contracts that are rigidly set up too early in a program, unless
they make provision for changes, are often counterproductive.
A badly written contract is a waste of time and money and,
when then used by managers to defend an indefensible
position, can do serious damage to business partnerships.

The rule must be that if you want a contract to protect your
business, go to an expert lawyer. Choose an expert in the
particular subject of contract law, and if it you have to take
legal action, get a lawyer who is also expert in the technical
subject covered in the contract. This will cost a lot of money, so
only use litigation as a last resort. Also remember that, unless
you have used such an expert to help you draft the contract in
the first place, you may have flaws in your documentation,
which could destroy your case.

## 18 MEET EXTRA TRAINING NEEDS

Managers and employees need special training to understand and cope with the additional risks and complexities of collaborative projects. In international collaborations, it is vital for all parties to recognize and respect each other's cultures to avoid the unintended insult, or the accidental misunderstanding, which can seriously damage progress.

You cannot expect your partners to always conform to your standards and practices. This approach will be seen as both insulting and patronizing. Careful training of all staff involved is necessary to minimize any such risks.

**benefits and risks of collaboration**

# Overview of benefits

- Improve buying power

- Share "after market" support costs

- Fill "gap" in resources

- Create larger pool of resources

- Share research and development costs

- Improve morale if handled well

- Take advantage of specialization opportunities

- Open new markets

Access "restricted" markets

Provide greater influence on market and regulations

Access better methods and processes

Increase financial resources and stability

Build a defensive wall

Pursue an aggressive strategy

Benefit from synergy

**OVERVIEW**

# Overview of risks

- Lose overall control of partnership project, or steamrollering

- Lose identity

- Lose company through Trojan Horse, or failure of partner

- Leave "holes" in projects

- Expose confidentiality issues

- Engage in communication and translation problems

- Work with different standards and procedures

- Lose in-house skills/expertise

- Lose technology know-how leadership

■ Deal with demands for extra priority and vigilance

■ Recognize cultural differences

■ Encounter adverse reactions of employees and trade unions

■ Get involved in monopolies and mergers issues

■ Assume accountability for failure

■ Keep on top of diverging company strategies

■ Recognize currency fluctuation and take on the cost of protection

■ Deal with inadequate/bad contractual agreements

■ Meet extra training needs

OVERVIEW

# Summary of benefits and risks

Though the number of benefits and risks listed in this chapter are very similar, the general consensus of the boards of directors of the vast majority of companies in both the advanced and developing worlds is that the financial and business value of the possible benefits far outweighs the risks.

Most modern businesses are rapidly developing and expanding their collaborative programs. This is particularly true of companies wishing to operate in the emerging international markets such as the Pacific Rim.

Companies involved in setting up and continuing successful collaborations develop a clear understanding of the risks in every area, adopt a pragmatic approach to the appointment and retention of high-quality staff to manage the collaboration in every territory, and recognize that the risks must be managed. All of these factors go some way toward minimizing their impact. In addition, if risks can be kept to a minimum, companies obtain the maximum competitive advantage from the many and varied benefits of a collaborative approach to business life.

# Is the time right for collaboration?

1    Is there still the possibility for internal growth? Check all internal procedures. ☐

2    Check the SWOT analysis to evaluate strengths and weaknesses. ☐

3    Could your strengths be an asset to your chosen partner? ☐

**4** Would your partner's projected strengths be a match for your weaknesses? ☐

**5** What resource match would be right for the current state of your business? ☐

**6** Can you protect your intellectual property? ☐

**7** What form of collaboration would be right at this point? ☐

CHECKLIST

# 6

planning for growth

# Innovation

We have looked at some of the ways that a business can grow, both by internal and external means. All of these are proven ways to enlarge the company and to enable your current activities to develop. But they must not be a haphazard choice.

Just as, at the beginning of the enterprise, a business plan was an essential ingredient of the start-up procedure, a growth plan is a vital tool to establish the way that the business can grow.

Ideas are the life-blood of any business. This does not only refer to new products but to improving the way that current products and services are produced, and improving the efficiency of the organization as it now exists. Phrases such as "lean production," "total quality," and "doing more with less" make us take a good look at the business and see whether there are any wasteful processes that will harm efficiency. They should encourage all members of the staff at every level of the organization to look at the jobs that they do and to see if they can be improved upon. Each employee's customer is the next person in the process in which they are involved, and it should be each employee's aim to keep his or her customer happy.

An important concept in the production of a growth plan is the idea of innovation. The word "innovation" means "to bring in new ideas and methods; to make changes." You need to use innovation to grow your business. It will improve profitability, and that will be the fuel that will enable the company to grow. It is important to create a working environment that will produce and nurture innovative ideas.

It is necessary to understand the difference between "invention" and "innovation." The former is the process that turns an idea into a reality. The latter is the successful exploitation of the idea.

Note: In planning for growth, the principles expressed in these pages can be applied to both manufacturing and service companies, with some exceptions, namely outsourcing. The risks and benefits outlined in Chapter 5 apply to both sectors.

# Innovation continued

Innovation could be the introduction of a totally new product or service into
the range offered to customers, or it could be some small but vital changes
to improve the product or to change the methods used in the manufacture
of your products. Whatever form it takes, it has to involve some creative
process. These creative ideas may come from a variety of sources:

**1** From inside the business via employees and managers.

**2** From your own in-house or an external research and
development organization.

**3** From suppliers suggesting new materials or processes to
improve the items they supply.

**4** From customers and market research that show where new
opportunities exist.

FROM THE EARLIER DEFINITION, THESE IDEAS WILL:

- improve your existing processes to induce greater efficiency and productivity

- add value to your existing products that will give an edge to your range

- extend the range of your products and services

- establish new partnerships

- improve profitability

- increase your customers and markets

Failure to innovate will have a detrimental effect on the business and will lead to falling productivity, loss of key staff who will seek other companies that appear to be more aggressive, reduced profits, and eventually the loss of the business. This is why innovation should be high in your growth plan.

# Employees

Each employee should be encouraged to look upon the next person in the process as his or her customer. Businesses often fail to recognize that their most valuable asset is their employees and that they can be the source of many innovative ideas. To enable them to feel valued and willing to contribute innovative ideas, you need to establish the right environment for creative thinking.

**1** Do your staff have the apparatus to enable them to submit ideas?

- Do you encourage "workers circles" at which staff can submit ideas to their peers and managers about how their job could be done more efficiently, and the effect it would have on others?

- Do you hold brainstorming sessions, either at the workplace or away from it where their ideas can be collected and discussed?

- Are there suggestion boxes into which ideas can be placed?

**2** Do you encourage an atmosphere that will support employees in freely expressing their ideas without ridicule from management and peers? It is surprising how often a simple idea, although not workable itself, can lead to other ideas that can be turned into new methods.

**3** Do you promote the idea that all employees share the responsibility for innovation? The one person who really knows how a task or process should be done is the person who is doing it. Have they been encouraged to suggest new or improved ways to do their jobs? What would be the reaction from the managers of their sections or departments if they made such suggestions? This aspect could prove to be one of the more productive elements of employee relations.

**4** Do you reward innovation? A reward for the best suggestion each month will certainly encourage participation even though the suggestion may not be capable of implementation. A panel of employees from all aspects of the business could decide upon the winning idea. Any ideas that are implemented and that result in significant cost savings should be rewarded with a bonus and should be publicized throughout the company.

# Customer feedback

Customers will, if asked, provide useful feedback on the performance and efficiency of the business.

**1** A successful business depends on giving customers what they want and expect.

**2** If the customer is not satisfied with the service or product that it receives, it will turn elsewhere for its requirements, so you have lost a customer.

**3** Customer satisfaction is a growth strategy, but do you know if your customers are really satisfied?

**4** Lack of complaints does not necessarily mean that customers are happy with your product.

**5** Dissatisfied customers often go elsewhere without necessarily complaining to you.

**6** Compile a questionnaire to send to customers. This will not only report on satisfaction but will also suggest ways in which your products or services can be improved.

**7** This is another innovation that will help to bring about a change to your business procedures and help the company to grow.

**planning for growth**

# Knowledge

It has been said that "knowledge is power": knowledge is certainly a powerful element in business growth.

**1** It is essential to know your staff, the product, your customers, and the business environment in which you operate.

**2** This will apply to all sizes of company from the largest multinational to the local store.

**3** It will be useful to look at each area in turn.

KNOW YOUR EMPLOYEES

**1** You have most probably selected your employees for the skill and experience that they can give to the business.

**2** Carefully chosen, they can be a major force in the running and control of the company.

**3** Do you know all that they are capable of giving to the business?

**4** Do you encourage them not only to use the talents that make them good at the jobs that they do but also to bring all their experience to the benefit of the company?

**5** It is utilizing these assets that could set you apart from your business competitors.

# Knowledge continued

KNOW YOUR PRODUCT

When the business was started you looked at the product from all aspects to ensure that it met the requirements of the marketplace.

**1** Does it still fulfil all that is required of it?

**2** Have the products of your competitors become more sought after than your own?

**3** If no one wanted your product, you would not still be in business so you must be doing something right, but what will give you that competitive edge that will make the business grow?

KNOW YOUR CUSTOMERS

We have already mentioned customer feedback and some of the ways that it can be obtained.

**1** It is now necessary to make use of this information.

**2** How do your customers use the product that you supply to them?

**3** Is it used in their production process, or is it built in to something that they make and supply?

**4** Can you target any of your customers with a tailor-made service of a specific type?

# Knowledge continued

KNOW YOUR BUSINESS ENVIRONMENT

Your business has to be aware of all the external influences that can play a part in its success or downfall.

**1** Undertake a SWOT analysis to establish the strengths and weakness of your organization (see pp. 26–27).

**2** It is also useful to conduct a PEST analysis (see pp. 30–33) to see the effect of external forces. PEST represents

■ Political

■ Economic

■ Social

■ Technological

A PEST analysis looks at how these forces will have an impact upon your business and help to determine the possibilities for growth.

LOOK AT PEST IN MORE DETAIL

### 1 POLITICAL

■ Look at what is happening at both national and international levels that might impact the way in which your business is able to operate.

■ New laws relating to trade, product liability, and product safety standards will determine your ability to trade both at home and abroad.

■ Ensure you are on all relevant mailing lists for governmental updates to keep you informed of latest developments.

### 2 ECONOMIC

■ The global economy affects the buying patterns of companies and individuals around the world and will affect your ability to sell in the established markets.

■ Attempting to predict economic trends before your competitors could enable you to fight off any possible market downturn.

## 3 SOCIAL

■ Social outlook changes over time, and the expectations of the public can have a major effect upon the desirability of the product that you supply.

■ Trends in fashion, not only in clothing but in the way people live will determine which products are marketable.

■ Environmental issues affect the way customers choose the products they buy.

■ Not all products are affected by social and environmental changes, but it is good business sense to take into account the knowledge obtained in these areas when considering the way in which your company can grow.

**4** TECHNOLOGICAL

■ We live in an age of technological advancement, some industries more so than others.

■ New inventions and innovative designs and ideas can render products obsolete almost overnight.

■ You need a sound knowledge of the likely advances in your industry to meet the requirements of the market to keep the business profitable.

■ You also need to "ride the wave" of technology to ensure that you stay ahead of the competition in order to grow.

The PEST analysis might show that you have sufficient strengths to meet these external challenges or expose weaknesses in your organization that must be remedied as soon as possible. A good knowledge database will prove invaluable in your planning for growth.

# Knowledge continued

There are other sources of knowledge that can be used to maintain your position in the market and to enable you to plan growth.

**1** The Internet has details of the economic trends of the industrial sector in which your business is placed.

**2** The business pages of on-line newsgroups highlight any problems that competitors may be experiencing.

**3** Professional associations and trade magazines publish the latest information on their member organizations, especially when the news is good and companies want it to be known.

**4** The converse can also be a useful guide.

One important thing to remember about knowledge is that it needs to be protected. There is no point in building up a vast database if it is allowed to leak away and benefit a competitor.

As it is an intangible asset, it needs protection under the laws concerning intellectual property. It can be protected by the regulations concerning patents, copyright, and confidentiality.

It is said, "it is not what you know but who you know that matters."

**1** Knowing the "right" people can be a great asset in planning for growth.

**2** Employing non-executive directors can enhance the capability of a company for they bring a wealth of business experience, gathered from many years in various companies.

**3** They can be from various backgrounds such as finance, marketing, or commerce. Their experience and expertise can prove invaluable when planning to grow your business.

# Outsourcing

Resources are usually finite, and making the best use of the resources that the business has is one of the skills that the manager has to acquire and use judiciously.

**1** With an unending supply of money in a business, the rate of growth would be quite phenomenal.

**2** As this is seldom the case, ways have to be found to make best use of all the resources at your disposal.

**3** In-house control of all elements of the business is desirable, but it is not always practicable.

**4** Many of the functions undertaken by the business may be performed more profitably by an outsider, thereby freeing scarcer resources to enable other work to be done internally, control of which should not be given to someone else.

**5** An example of the work that can be profitably outsourced, especially in a small company, is the payroll function.

**6** Functions such as accounting, PR, and recruitment can also be successfully outsourced.

# Outsourcing continued

Outsourcing enables your business to do what it does best, it can save you money and allow more flexibility.

**1** It needs to be controlled, and it requires a policy.

**2** This policy is sometimes called the "make-or-buy" decision, in which you have to decide if, in the long term, more benefit can be obtained from either choice.

**3** The best time to decide on the route to follow is when new projects are planned and before money is spent in buying more plant and machinery or employing skilled workers to produce the items.

**4** In many cases, the utilization of machinery can be as low as 20–25 percent, and justification must be found before large investments are made.

**5** Owning the latest computer-controlled machines may be good for the ego, but it is anathema for the balance sheet.

# Outsourcing continued

Before making a decision, costs must be carefully assessed to see if there are savings to be made.

**1** Will the benefits really outweigh the risks?

**2** Having made the decision to outsource, the process will have to be carefully managed and controlled.

**3** Although the work has been given to a supplier, responsibility must still remain in-house and regular progress established.

**4** Treat the chosen supplier as an added resource. Do not trade at "arm's length" but develop a partnership.

**5** Finding the right partner is not easy, and the initial work you put into establishing the right choice will use up valuable time and resources.

**6** These costs must be calculated into the equation for cost advantages.

**7** Go for a long-term relationship as the initial costs are then spread over a significant quantity of items, thereby making them more cost-effective.

**8** Also remember that your customers will still hold you responsible for quality and delivery, so your chosen partner must not damage these in any way.

**9** Ensure that control remains with you by setting the terms initially in a contract.

**10** Try to outsource several items so that you can employ one person to manage all of the partners and to act as a contact in case of problems.

# Management

Managing a business as it grows is like the plate-spinning act, where the performer spins plates on top of flexible poles and tries to keep the plates moving as he adds more plates without the existing plates falling.

**1** However multiskilled you are, if you do not plan and build a management team and have them in situ before the expansion takes place, you run the risk of being like the plate spinner, constantly running around.

**2** In fact, the team, correctly chosen, can help to plan and promote the growth of the business.

**3** Not only will each member of the team bring his or her own field of expertise to benefit the business, but they will combine all of the skills to give a wider view of the proposed expansion.

**4** It is vital to factor in the staff costs of having a management team in place—this should always be included in your cash flow projection.

planning for growth

# Choosing the team

Before employing or promoting anyone for the management team, it is necessary to have given some thought to the roles that they need to have.

**1** Areas of expertise are discussed on pp. 224–225.

**2** Their professional expertise is just as important as the way in which they relate to other members of the team.

**3** There will need to be a rapport between members to ensure harmonious working relationships.

**4** Dr. R. Meredith Belbin, in his theory on team roles, postulates that there are nine different team roles and that a mixture of these roles should appear in all functioning groups.

**5** Most members can fill two roles, and it is in achieving the right balance that the team is most effective. Team roles can and do change over time, in response to internal and external factors.

# Areas of expertise

Depending on the type of business, the following are the most likely functions that will need a dedicated manager:

**1** Sales and marketing

**2** Production

**3** Finance

**4** Administration

**5** Procurement

The type of business and the chosen path of growth will determine which of these departments are most necessary and the time scale in which they can be introduced. It could be that any of these functions could be outsourced, but it will be beneficial to have the service provider available for the management meetings where future plans will be discussed.

As a help in deciding which areas are necessary at the present time and to determine your relative strengths and weaknesses, refer to the SWOT analysis that you prepared earlier and that has been regularly updated.

# Training

Before placing a recruitment advertisement, have you assessed the potential of your current staff to see if any have the right background or skills to fill the roles required?

**1** Does anyone show management potential but lack technical expertise?

**2** Are there staff who are experts at their job but could benefit from management training?

**3** There are numerous courses available to teach all the skills required to produce a fully qualified employee who can fill the position needed.

**4** Training should be regarded as an investment in the future of both the employee and the company.

**5** Suitable training courses may be found through word of mouth or via the Internet.

**6** It is often possible to organize a trainer to come into your premises to run a course for a number of employees at the same time.

# Financing growth

The method that your business chooses to finance planned growth will depend above all on the type of operation that you are running.

For example, a public limited company will most probably seek to issue more stock to be able to expand, or it may seek to arrange loans to cover the interim period between expansion and the returns that such increased trade should bring.

A partnership or sole trader may have to rely upon themselves, family, or friends to fund the planned growth. This could depend on the success of the business so far and the projected return on investment.

If the planned growth is gradual, it may be possible to fund from savings that are made from running a more efficient organization, but this could take longer than the competition will allow.

There is also the possibility of raising a bank loan, but this could depend upon your financial standing, as banks are sometimes unwilling to lend to customers they classify as overcommitted.

A larger business with good prospects might attract outside investors. These are sometimes known as "business angels" and may be willing to invest in exchange for a share in the business.

In some countries, it may be possible to qualify for a grant, either from central or regional government. This is usually dependent upon the area that the business is located, preferably one designated a "regeneration area."

It might be necessary to use a mixture of these sources to raise the total amount required. As was mentioned in a previous chapter, collaborating with financial institutions is one of the benefits that should be exploited where possible.

Whatever the chosen method, the precursor must be a detailed business plan and a cash flow forecast. Both of these must be realistic and look at the worst case as well as the most optimistic outcome.

# Writing a business plan

As you may want to use your business plan to show to potential investors, the plan needs to be updated regularly. It should include:

**1** A statement of your business objectives.

**2** A brief outline of the birth of the business.

**3** A statement of where the business is headed.

**4** Time scales for achieving growth, both internal and external.

**5** Your marketing aims and objectives.

**6** The anticipated size of your projected market.

**7** Details of your operations, for example, your premises, plant, machinery, and supplier base.

**8** Financial information, including profit and loss forecasts, cash flow, and sales forecasts.

**9** Audited accounts where available.

# Writing a business plan continued

If your business has grown and has several departments or divisions, a
business plan for each separate area will ensure that you keep track of the
individual divisions as well as the business as a whole.

**1** This will allow each department head to monitor progress
within the overall plan.

**2** It will allow you as the head to see that targets are met.

**3** It will highlight any remedial action that needs to be taken.

**4** Departmental plans need to be more detailed than the master business plan.

**5** It will allow transfer of funds from one department to another, when necessary.

**6** It enables you to monitor costs between departments. For example, is one department ordering more stationery than all the others, or running up a huge telephone bill?

# Writing a cash flow projection

The cash flow forecast is a very important guide to your financial viability. It is often forgotten that in any type of manufacturing or service business costs have to be incurred before income is received.

A spreadsheet program will provide a good base for a cash flow forecast. The following items are essential for a preliminary chart, but further items can be added as the business grows. Months or financial periods should be entered across the page and cost headings recorded down the left side.

SOME OF THE HEADINGS MUST INCLUDE:

**1** Income, both from sales and capital (loans, shareholders funds, profits, etc.).

**2** Finance repayments and interest.

**3** Direct costs, both materials and direct labor.

**4** Expenses, which should include salaries, rent, and telephone.

BELOW THESE SHOULD BE TOTALS UNDER THE HEADINGS:

**1** Opening balance

**2** Income

**3** Expenditure

**4** Cash flow

**5** Closing balance

These figures will show how long it will take before the business starts to generate any profit. Be prepared for the shock of minus balances at the start. This will show if sufficient finance has been provided to enable you to carry on with the business.

# Index